JUANITA HIGH SCHOOL
10601 N.E. 132ND ST.
KIRKLAND, WA 98034

12 SUPER-INCREDIBLE DINOSAURS
YOU NEED TO KNOW

by Sonja Olson

www.12StoryLibrary.com

12-Story Library is an imprint of Peterson Publishing Company and Press Room Editions.

Produced for 12-Story Library by Red Line Editorial

Photographs ©: Elena Duvernay/Shutterstock Images, cover, 1, 17, 29; Kostyantyn Ivanyshen/Shutterstock Images, 4; Elena Duvernay/iStockphoto, 5, 19; Dorling Kindersley/ Thinkstock, 6, 7, 9, 10, 22, 24; Funkynusayri CC 3.0, 8; Corey Ford/iStockphoto, 11, 28; MR1805/iStockphoto, 12, 13, 16, 18, 20, 26; Daderot, 15; Russell Shively/Shutterstock Images, 21; Richard Ward/Thinkstock, 23; Alan Male/Thinkstock, 25; danefromspain/ Thinkstock, 27

ISBN
978-1-63235-139-5 (hardcover)
978-1-63235-181-4 (paperback)
978-1-62143-233-3 (hosted ebook)

Library of Congress Control Number: 2015934277

Printed in the United States of America
Mankato, MN
June, 2015

Go beyond the book. Get free, up-to-date content on this topic at 12StoryLibrary.com.

TABLE OF CONTENTS

1

THE BRACHIOSAURUS REACHED FOR THE TREETOPS

The Brachiosaurus holds the record for being the largest living thing to walk on Earth. Unlike other dinosaurs that could run on two legs, the Brachiosaurus needed four thick legs to support the weight of its body. Early illustrations showed the Brachiosaurus on its two back legs eating leaves from treetops. Scientists now believe the front legs held most of the weight. The two back legs were not strong enough to hold the dinosaur up.

The Brachiosaurus had a long neck. It was the tallest herbivore of its time. It could reach more than twice as high as a giraffe. The long neck was a problem for young Brachiosaurus. Since they were shorter, the neck was

There was no need for the Brachiosaurus to stretch to reach trees.

50

Height, in feet (15 m), of a tree that a Brachiosaurus could reach.

Pronounced: BRAK-ee-oh-sore-us

When: 155–140 million years ago, Late Jurassic Period

Fossil location: United States

Size: 50 feet (15 m) tall, 120,000 pounds (54,431 kg)

THINK ABOUT IT

Why was the slow-moving Brachiosaurus safe from attack once it was an adult? Why is traveling in herds safer than traveling alone?

easier for predators to bite and pull the dinosaur down. Once a Brachiosaurus was at its full height and weight, it was intimidating to most other dinosaurs and would have been difficult to attack and kill. Brachiosaurus are also believed to have lived and moved in herds. Healthy Brachiosaurus would have protected the younger or weaker Brachiosaurus from attack.

The Brachiosaurus had spoon-shaped teeth. This helped it eat through pinecones and ferns. The Brachiosaurus needed a lot of food each day. It ate 440 pounds (200 kg) of leaves and twigs every day.

The Brachiosaurus is recognizable by the lump on its forehead.

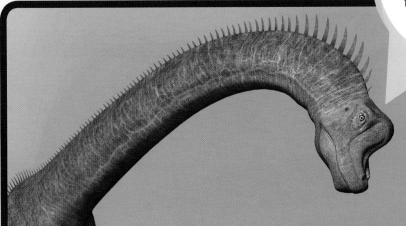

THE EORAPTOR WAS A SMALL BUT FIERCE PREDATOR

A small dinosaur ran through the river valley. It was the Eoraptor and it was one of the earliest dinosaurs discovered. It may have had scales or feathers covering its body. The Eoraptor's back legs were supported by its strong thighbones and muscles. Scientists know this dinosaur was a fast and strong hunter.

The Eoraptor was a carnivore. It ate small animals such as lizards and other reptiles. The Eoraptor may have also hunted larger animals by attacking them with its sharp claws and teeth. The Eoraptor could not hold onto larger prey so it would attack and then retreat and wait for

The Eoraptor ran on its back legs.

1

Number of complete
Eoraptor fossils that
have been found.

Pronounced: EE-oh-RAP-
tor
When: 230–225 million
years ago, Triassic
Period
Fossil location: Argentina
Size: 1 foot (0.3 m) tall,
20 pounds (9.1 kg)

the prey to weaken. Once the prey
collapsed, the Eoraptor would eat it.

Although it seems small with a
body only three feet (0.9 m) long,
it was large compared to some
other dinosaurs at the time. The
Eoraptor had sharp saw-like teeth
and claws. It also had large arm
muscles and could walk on its back
legs. Scientists believe the Eoraptor
was an ancestor of the fierce
Tyrannosaurus rex.

DR. ROBERT BAKKER

Dinosaurs were once thought
to be slow-moving reptiles that
dragged their tails when they
walked. Dr. Robert Bakker was
one of the first paleontologists
to change that image. He
compared dinosaurs with
modern-day animals. Bakker
argued that the Eoraptor and
other dinosaurs were intelligent,
quick-moving, and adaptable
creatures. He has become
one of the most famous
paleontologists as a result of
his theory.

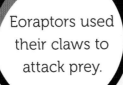

Eoraptors used
their claws to
attack prey.

MAIASAURA BUILT NESTS FOR THEIR YOUNG

In the 1970s, paleontologists in Choteau, Montana, found several bowl-shaped nests close together. They also found fossils of eggshells and skeletons of both young and adult dinosaurs. This may have been a nesting colony of the Maiasaura.

A nesting colony is when groups of parents live near to each other to raise their young.

A mother Maiasaura laid her eggs in a nest. Then she

Young Maiasaura needed their parents for food and protection.

DINOSAURS IN SPACE

A Maiasaura was the first dinosaur to go into space! In 1985, astronaut Loren Acton took fossils of an infant Maiasaura and eggshell pieces with him onto Spacelab 2. The NASA mission lasted eight days. The Maiasaura became the first dinosaur to orbit the earth. These fossils can now be seen at the Museum of the Rockies in Bozeman, Montana.

10,000

Number of Maiasaura fossils found together in Montana.

Pronounced: my-ah-SORE-ah

When: 80–74 million years ago, Cretaceous Period

Fossil location: United States

Size: 15 feet (4.6 m) tall, 8,000 pounds (3,629 kg)

egg fossils alongside hatchlings, juveniles, and adult Maiasaura fossils. Finding these fossils together leads paleontologists to believe the hatchlings stayed in the nest for at least one year or more. The parents cared for them. This is similar to birds that take care of their young.

Young Maiasaura did not have strong enough legs or teeth to leave the nest. They could not search for food to eat. Adult Maiasaura used their teeth to grind food for themselves and their young. Maiasaura ate gingko leaves, berries, and plant seeds.

covered them with leaves and dirt. When the baby Maiasaura hatched, they would dig themselves out of the nest. Sometimes the parents helped. Scientists have found Maiasaura

The Maiasaura's name means "good mother lizard."

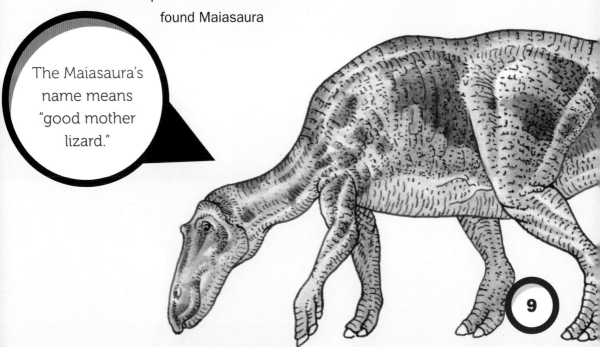

PARASAUROLOPHUS MADE A FOGHORN SOUND

A foghorn-like sound was heard in the woodlands of North America. The noise came from the Parasaurolophus. On top of its head was a crest running from the front to the back. The crest had hollow tubes inside. Scientists believe air blew through these tubes. It made a sound.

The Parasaurolophus used its foghorn-like call to communicate with other Parasaurolophus.

The Parasaurolophus had a stout muscular body with big shoulders. This helped it push through bushes in the deep forests where it lived. It also had strong back legs. It could walk or run on two legs. Its strong legs helped it run quickly. The Parasaurolophus could run up to 25 miles per hour (40 km/h).

The Parasaurolophus ate pine needles and twigs. It also may have eaten tree leaves. It would have cut leaves off the tree with its sharp beak. Then hundreds of teeth in

6.5

Length, in feet (2 m), of the Parasaurolophus's head crest.

Pronounced: pa-ra-saw-ROL-off-us

When: 76–74 million years ago, Late Cretaceous Period

Fossil location: Canada, United States

Size: 16 feet (4.9 m) tall, 6,000–8,000 pounds (2,722–3,629 kg)

its cheeks would have ground the leaves into small pieces.

The Parasaurolophus had great eyesight and hearing. This helped it survive. It did not have claws, spikes, or thick skin like other herbivores to protect against predators.

Parasaurolophus lived in herds.

QUETZALCOATLUS SWOOPED FROM THE SKIES

The Quetzalcoatlus was one of the largest flying animals. It was a pterosaur. A pterosaur was not a dinosaur but a flying reptile. Its wings were formed from skin stretched between the leg and a long finger bone. This flying reptile was the size of an adult giraffe. The Quetzalcoatlus had light bones to help it fly despite its size.

Paleontologists have a lot of questions about the

The Quetzalcoatlus's wingspan was wider than a tennis court!

Quetzalcoatlus. They do not know if it flew by flapping its wings or by gliding from high cliffs. They also are unsure if it spent most of its day in the sky. Some paleontologists believe the flying reptile stalked prey by walking on its legs.

Some scientists believe the Quetzalcoatlus spent some time on land.

Paleontologists do agree that the Quetzalcoatlus was a carnivore. They do not agree on what it ate. Some think it flew down from the sky to scoop up fish. Others think it was too large to hunt while flying and hunted small dinosaurs on land. Others think it ate dead animals.

DINOSAUR NAMES

The Quetzalcoatlus is named after the ancient Aztec god, Quetzalcoatl. Quetzalcoatl translates to "feathered serpent." It was a good description of the pterosaur when the fossils were first discovered in 1971. Dinosaurs are usually named after a physical feature or the location where they are found. They are rarely named after the paleontologists who discovered their fossils.

30

Length, in feet (9.1 m), of the Quetzalcoatlus's wingspan.

Pronounced: KWET-zal-koh-AT-lus
When: 70–65 million years ago, Cretaceous Period
Fossil location: United States
Size: 18 feet (5.5 m) tall, 220 pounds (100 kg)

SINORNITHOSAURUS SHOWED OFF COLORFUL FEATHERS

In 1999, a complete Sinornithosaurus skeleton was discovered in China and named "Dave." By studying Dave and other fossils, scientists know the Sinornithosaurus was covered in feathers of different colors and sizes. This discovery was important. The Sinornithosaurus was one of the first creatures on Earth to have feathers.

The body was covered in fluffy feathers to keep heat in. Even though the Sinornithosaurus was covered in feathers, it was not a true bird. It could not fly, but it was excellent at climbing trees.

The Sinornithosaurus was a carnivore that hunted small animals, birds, and dinosaurs. Some paleontologists believe the dinosaur was also venomous. In 2009, a well-preserved Sinornithosaurus skull was found. The long, pointed teeth had grooves in them much like a venomous snake. They also found a cavity, or empty space, in the jaw that could have been a venom gland.

One year later another study was done by a different group of paleontologists. They believed grooved teeth had been found in

6.5

Length, in feet (2 m), of the Sinornithosaurus.

Pronounced: SINE-or-nith-oh-sore-rus
When: 130–125 million years ago, Early Cretaceous Period
Fossil location: China
Size: 18 inches (46 cm) tall, 20 pounds (9.1 kg)

THINK ABOUT IT

What methods would you use to determine whether or not the Sinornithosaurus was venomous? How would the study of modern animals and reptiles help you? Why do you think there is not more agreement among paleontologists on the biology and behavior of dinosaurs?

other nonvenomous dinosaurs. The grooves were a result of normal wear and tear throughout the dinosaur's life. Paleontologists are still looking for a clear answer on whether the Sinornithosaurus was the first venomous dinosaur or not.

Paleontologists were able to learn a lot by finding the Sinornithosaurus fossil.

SPINOSAURUS SENSED MOVEMENT WITH SNOUT

While the Tyrannosaurus rex may be more famous, the Spinosaurus holds the title for the largest land-dwelling carnivore of all time. In addition to its size, the Spinosaurus is most recognized for the sail running down its back. Its spine supported the sail. Paleontologists are unsure exactly of the spiny sail's purpose. It could have been to adjust body temperature, to store body fat, or to attract a mate.

The Spinosaurus had a long snout and clawed hands. Its strong arms were built to catch large fish. It may have had pressure sensors in

The spine on the Spinosaurus was as tall as a grown man.

its snout that helped it sense movement in the water. The Spinosaurus could catch fish without even seeing them! It was a good swimmer but was also skilled at hunting on land. The Spinosaurus was very quick both on land and in water.

Some scientists believe the Spinosaurus spent most of its time in the water.

Pronounced: SPINE-oh-SORE-us

When: 112–97 million years ago, Late Cretaceous Period

Fossil location: Egypt, Libya, Morocco

Size: 16 feet (4.9 m) tall, 24,000 pounds (10,886 kg)

STEGOSAURUS DEFENDED ITSELF WITH SPIKY TAIL

At 14 feet (4.3 m) tall and 30 feet (9.1 m) long, the Stegosaurus was an impressive sight. The herbivore had a double row of plates running down its neck, back, and tail. These plates made the dinosaur look bigger and more threatening. The plates did not protect the Stegosaurus though. They attracted the attention of a possible mate. The Stegosaurus used small rounded bones for defense. These bones covered the throat and protected the dinosaur during an

The Stegosaurus could swing its tail back and forth in defense.

attack. The tail also had spikes on the tip.

The low position of the head forced the dinosaur to eat low-growing plants. The Stegosaurus tore leaves with its beak. In the back of the mouth, teeth crushed the leaves. Then the Stegosaurus swallowed and the leaves were further broken down in the digestive system.

The Stegosaurus brain was very small. Paleontologists found a large empty area of the spinal cord at the hip area. This led people to believe the Stegosaurus had two brains. Some believe the first brain controlled body functions such as keeping the heart beating and digesting food. The second brain

would have controlled walking and how the dinosaur held and moved its tail. This theory is still under debate.

17

Number of plates the Stegosaurus had from its back to its tail.

Pronounced: STEG-oh-SORE-us

When: 150–145 million years ago, Late Jurassic Period

Fossil location: Portugal, United States

Size: 14 feet (4.3 m) tall, 6,000 pounds (2,722 kg)

The Stegosaurus drank and ate from the ground because it was easier to reach food there.

STENOPTERYGIUS SURPRISED ITS NEXT MEAL

Swimming in prehistoric waters, the Stenopterygius darted quickly to catch fish. It looked and acted very similar to modern-day dolphins. Its body was smooth, and its muscular back fin pushed it through the water. It would storm into a school of fish and quickly use its long, tooth-filled

The Stenopterygius was a very fast swimmer.

snout to eat the confused fish. The Stenopterygius could swim as fast as 60 miles per hour (97 km/h) and strike with little warning. In addition to fish, it ate animals such as prehistoric squid.

The Stenopterygius was a marine reptile, or ichthyosaur, not a dinosaur. Unlike most marine reptiles, it did not crawl onto dry land to lay eggs. The Stenopterygius gave birth to live young. Fossils show females giving birth and the young coming out tail first. After birth, the babies lived without their mother's care and were fully independent.

60

Speed, in miles per hour (97 km/h), the Stenopterygius could swim.

Pronounced: STEN-oh-ter-IH-gee-us

When: 206–144 million years ago, Jurassic Period

Fossil location: Argentina, France, Germany, Great Britain

Size: 6 feet (1.8 m) long, 100–200 pounds (45–91 kg)

Very few fossils of the Stenopterygius have been found.

TRICERATOPS FOUGHT OTHER DINOSAURS WITH HORNS

The three-horned Triceratops had a short nose horn and two longer horns on its forehead. Behind the brow horns was a large frill. It is believed to have helped regulate body temperature. The horns and frill are thought to be used to attract mates. The horns grew back if broken or worn down. Paleontologists have found bite marks from the Tyrannosaurus rex on the skulls of Triceratops. Another skull was missing one brow horn.

The neck was very flexible and Triceratops could feed on tree leaves as well as low-growing plants in the woodlands where it lived. It used its

Paleontologists believe the horns may have served as protection and defense in battles.

PALEONTOLOGISTS' WORK

Paleontologists are not finished studying dinosaurs. Once a study is published, it is examined and re-examined. Not everyone always agrees with the findings. More and more information is added as scientists learn about these extinct creatures. Through further studies of the fossils, it is believed that the Triceratops is not an individual species of dinosaur. It may actually be a juvenile Torosaurus.

beak to cut off leaves and plants such as ferns and palms. Its scissor-like teeth would cut up the plants before swallowing.

The Triceratops's skull was very solid and more than six feet (1.8 m) long. The thickness of the skulls has allowed them to fossilize better than other dinosaur skulls. More than 50 Triceratops skulls have been found.

3

Length, in feet (0.91 m), of the Triceratops's brow horn.

Pronounced: tri-SER-ra-tops

When: 70–65 million years ago, Late Cretaceous Period

Fossil location: United States

Size: 9.5 feet (2.9 m) tall, 14,000 pounds (6,350 kg)

The frill of the Triceratops was made of bone.

23

TYRANNOSAURUS REX USED SHARP TEETH TO CAPTURE PREY

The Tyrannosaurus rex may be the most feared and most famous of all dinosaurs. While it was the biggest dinosaur of the Cretaceous Period, it was not the biggest carnivore in dinosaur history. The Spinosaurus and Giganotosaurus were taller and weighed more but were not alive at the same time.

Most carnivores have knife-like teeth with saw-toothed edges. The Tyrannosaurus rex had spiky teeth that were pointed backward to hold in their prey. The teeth could pierce through skin, muscles, and bone. Smaller prey was shaken apart. Larger prey was injured. Worn tooth tips and bone fragments have been found in fossilized feces.

This means the Tyrannosaurus rex crushed and swallowed bones while eating the entire animal. The shape of its teeth, along with a huge, strong jaw has led some paleontologists to think the Tyrannosaurus rex was a scavenger and a predator.

The Tyrannosaurus rex was as long as one school bus and had a strong bite.

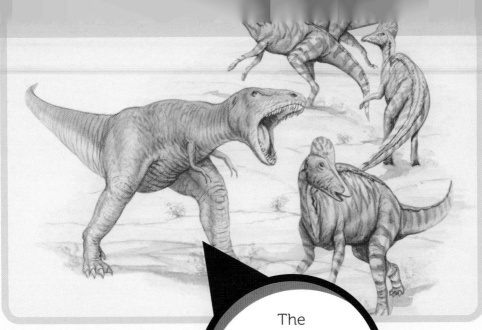

The Tyrannosaurus rex's body shape allowed it to run to catch smaller dinosaurs.

The Tyrannosaurus rex's short forearms were not long enough to reach its mouth. The arms may have been used to hold the prey and keep it from struggling free. The Tyrannosaurus rex had long, back legs and slender ankles. The Tyrannosaurus rex had to be careful while running because a fall could be deadly for a dinosaur that size.

THINK ABOUT IT

How did the Tyrannosaurus rex capture its prey? What special features did it have to keep the prey from escaping?

30
Number of incomplete fossils that have been found of the Tyrannosaurus rex.

Pronounced: tie-RAN-oh-SORE-us REX

When: 70–65 million years ago, Late Cretaceous Period

Fossil location: Canada, United States

Size: 13 feet (4 m) tall, 16,000 pounds (7,257 kg)

VELOCIRAPTOR WRESTLED ITS PREY

The Velociraptor became famous in the movie *Jurassic Park*. In reality, the dinosaurs were half the size of the ones shown in the movie. The Velociraptor was approximately the size of a wolf. It was slim and covered in feathers. Although no feathered fossils have been found, quill nodes have been found. Quill nodes are small bumps where feathers would be anchored. The feathers could have regulated temperature. This led paleontologists to believe Velociraptors were warm-blooded birds. They did

Although it was covered in feathers, the Velociraptor could not fly.

RAPTORS

The term *raptor* means "thief." But not all dinosaurs with this name are true raptors. In the 1920s, a nest of dinosaur eggs was found buried in the sands of the Gobi Desert. Nearby, paleontologists found the skeleton of the mother but thought it was a different species. They named the mother Oviraptor, meaning "egg thief." The paleontologists originally thought she was there to steal and eat the eggs. Even when they discovered she was the mother, the name stuck.

The Velociraptor had huge toe claws it used to attack predators.

not have wings and were too heavy for their size to be able to take flight.

The Velociraptor had clawed arms that unfolded like wings. The arms wrestled down prey such as lizards, mammals, and small dinosaurs. A complete skeleton of a Velociraptor was found fighting a Protoceratops. The two dinosaurs died while fighting and were eventually buried in a sandstorm.

20

Speed, in miles per hour (30 km/h), the Velociraptor could run.

- Pronounced: vel-OSS-ee-rap-tor
- When: 85 million years ago, Late Cretaceous Period
- Fossil location: China, Mongolia, Russia
- Size: 2.5 feet (0.76 m) tall, 200 pounds (91 kg)

27

FACT SHEET

- Dinosaurs are reptiles that lived on land, laid eggs, and walked on two or four legs.

- Pterosaurs (flying reptiles) and ichthyosaurs (marine reptiles) were alive at the same time as dinosaurs.

- Pterosaurs were the first vertebrates to be able to fly.

- Dinosaurs are extinct, meaning there are no species of dinosaurs living today. No one knows for sure why they became extinct.

- Most scientists agree that birds have descended from meat-eating dinosaurs.

- The Mesozoic Era began 245 million years ago and lasted for 180 million years. It is sometimes called the Age of Reptiles and is divided into three periods: the Triassic, Jurassic, and Cretaceous.

- Dinosaurs began to emerge in the late Triassic Period. Primitive dinosaurs were smaller in size and slowly became larger. The climate was very hot.

- The Jurassic Period was the age of the giant dinosaurs. At no other time were dinosaurs so large and so diverse. The climate was humid and warm.

- Dinosaurs dominated prehistoric life in the Cretaceous Period. It was during this period that dinosaurs became extinct. The climate varied between warm and cold.

- Many people assume dinosaurs were cold-blooded because modern day reptiles are.

GLOSSARY

ancestor
An early animal from which a modern animal developed.

carnivore
A meat eater.

extinct
No longer existing.

frill
Thick hair, feathers, bone, or cartilage around the neck.

hatchling
A very young animal that has just come from the egg.

herbivore
A plant eater.

juvenile
A young or undeveloped human or animal.

paleontologist
A scientist who studies fossils to learn about ancient life.

prey
An animal that is hunted or killed by another for food.

regulate
To fix or adjust the degree of something.

scavenger
An animal that feeds on dead animals, dead plant matter, and trash.

venomous
Capable of putting poison into another animal's body.

warm–blooded
Maintaining a constant body temperature.

FOR MORE INFORMATION

Books

Dinosaurs: A Visual Encyclopedia. New York: DK Publishing, 2013.

Dinosaurs: Uncover the Prehistoric World! New York: Parragon, 2013.

Palmer, Douglas. *Prehistoric Life: The Definitive Visual History of Life on Earth.* New York: DK Publishing, 2009.

Yates, Adam. *Guide to Wild Dinosaurs.* New York: Sterling, 2002.

Websites

BBC Earth: Spinosaurus
www.bbcearth.com/walking-with-dinosaurs/modal/spinosaurus

The Dinosaur Society
www.dinosaursociety.com/news

Discovery News: Dinosaurs
www.news.discovery.com/animals/dinosaurs

INDEX

About the Author

Sonja Olson is an author, artist, and teacher living in Saint Paul, Minnesota. She has a masters in education from the University of St. Thomas and works as a Montessori preschool teacher.